The Craft Fair Vendor Guidebook:

Ideas to Inspire

Printed in the
United States of America

Dedication

This book is dedicated to my husband Don
who has to share an office space with my crafting clutter
and loves me anyway.

Books by Brenda DeHaan

The Craft Fair Vendor Guidebook: Ideas to Inspire

Crafty Decluttering

ISBN: 9781973574774

DeHaan, Brenda.
Craft Fair Vendor Guidebook: Ideas to Inspire
1. Crafts and hobbies. 2. Home-based businesses. 3. Vendor displays. 4. Handicrafts.
5. Marketing. 6. Entrepreneurship 7. Jewelry
745.5

Table of Contents

Craft Fair Vendor Guidebook: Ideas to Inspire shares my experiences to help other people from newbies to veteran vendors. My specialty is wire-wrapped necklaces, but many of the book's economical display ideas and tips will work for various types of products.

I started wire-wrapping tumbled semi-precious gemstones in November 2011, opened my Rockin' Crystals Etsy store in January 2012, and had my first craft fair with my jewelry in March 2012. This book also includes options beyond craft and vendor fairs.

When it comes to display ideas, pictures explain more than words; therefore, this book is a "picture book for adults" to spark ideas to enhance your own booths. I photographed various vendor events before I realized that I would be putting them in a book; they are my reality, crooked chains and all!

I continue to learn from every craft fair and am definitely not an expert. I live in a small town in a rural state, so things may be different where you live. My lessons are here for you to utilize and adapt to your craft or direct sales business.

Enjoy!

Business basics

✓ First, you need a business name. Ideally, it should reflect your type of product. Search online to see if other businesses have the same name.

✓ After you have decided on a name, it's time to apply for a sales tax number. Look online (or ask a librarian) to find where to apply in your state. At each show, you will be given a form to be mailed afterwards to the Department of Revenue.

✓ Buy a receipt book or use an electronic system appropriate for your business.

✓ Next, order business cards and a debit/credit card reader.

✓ A prominent sign is good marketing. More on this will be explained later.

Find your venues

● Ask other vendors about their upcoming shows.

● Join Facebook groups for crafts/vendors. Just search for "craft fair vendor shows" in your state and request becoming a member. These sites post information about upcoming shows, whom to contact, and other details.

● Network with friends to tag you in upcoming events.

● Decide if the booth fee and travel expenses will be offset by sales. Bigger events have more traffic, but they have more competition also. Smaller shows closer to home may be more profitable.

● Write shows on your calendar and add them to your phone's calendar.

● Take pictures of each show's vendor application. It's easy to check your phone's photos for information if you need to refresh your memory on the show's details, especially the set-up times.

Types of venues

❖ **Craft fair:** All items must be made or constructed by the seller.
   *NOTE: For simplicity's sake, this book mainly uses the term **craft fair** in its more generic meaning of shows where people sell handmade or purchased items, technically a...* ⟩

❖ **Craft and vendor show:** Crafters and vendors of direct sales or commercial products are welcome. If customers come for handcrafted items, you have less competition at these shows, yet the direct sales people pull in additional people.

❖ **Holistic health expo:** Targeted at people interested in natural, holistic products and services, these events are usually held in cities. I travel from 2-6 hours to have a booth. My necklaces are made with semiprecious gemstones which are considered healing crystals, and I really enjoy the energy at holistic health venues. Booth fees are sometimes over $125, but the events have speakers and activities, so the guests spend several hours (or days) there and visit the vendor booths multiple times.

❖ **Artists' market:** Handcrafted, artistic, one-of-a-kind items are expected. If it's a juried show, you must submit photos or evidence of your work to first be accepted as a possible vendor.

❖ **Ladies' Night Out:** In my area, this is a promotion usually on a Thursday or Friday from 4-8 p.m. Businesses stay open, vendors set up in a designated location, and it's geared toward working women. Refreshments are served. One neighboring town concluded their event by showing a "chick flick" at the community's theatre. You had to be an adult woman to attend, and free wine was served. *Cheers!*

❖ **Pop up shops:** Vendors set up a temporary shop, usually inside of an established business. If space allows, you could have a pop-up shop with vendor friends to attract an even larger crowd.

Set up a pop up shop in a retail store for a win-win.

❖ **Indoor vs. outdoor:** Many summer shows are outdoors. Get ready for potential heat, cold, wind, rain...or perfect weather! Helpful supplies include a shade canopy and a fan.

Banners

My first sign was a vinyl banner with a horizontal layout and grommets for hanging. The trick was figuring out *how* to hang it. I used an ivory curtain panel with grommets and two gigantic decorative "paper clips" to attach the banner. When hanging in front of your booth, a sign is not visible when people are standing by it. Furthermore, it was difficult getting the horizontal banner to hang right. It worked with a little finagling, but then I splurged!

After four years I switched to a 6' retractable vinyl vertical banner. It cost over $100, but has been much easier to use and makes quite a statement! The company had two price options. Customer service explained that the higher priced banner had higher resolution which was worth the extra $20 to me.

I designed the banner with a photograph of one of my favorite necklaces. The enlarged azurite with malachite necklace resembles the world.

Since I hear potential customers say, "I already have so many necklaces," my slogan is "One can never have too many necklaces."

Really, how much space does one necklace take?

Preparing and packing

Set up at home before your first show of the season and take pictures to remind yourself how you'd arranged everything. This picture was taken before my first show in 2012. I used two vintage purple bridesmaid dresses. One show with those was enough. (OK, more than enough!)

Create and save a packing list.

You will take basically the same things to every show, so keep your list and check it more than twice.

Get some money, honey!

Many people pay with $20 bills, but they appreciate being able to use their debit/credit cards. Some want to pay with $100 bills, but they are the exception. It'd be one thing if they wanted to purchase over $50 worth of merchandise; it's another thing when they want to buy an $18 item with a $100 bill at the beginning of your show.

I usually start with $80-$100 in change with mainly small bills.

$1 and $5 bills and a debit/credit card reader will be utilized the most.

8

An economical, portable jewelry display case

After looking for quite a while, I finally found folding wood jewelry display cases for over $100 online. I needed 4 cases, and $400 was beyond my budget.

I thought of a way to make some for approximately **$20** each. I bought four art kits meant for beginning artists. This resulted in a lot of art supplies that I didn't need, but I knew someone who did. Extra supplies could be donated to art or regular classroom teachers, Girl Scouts, Boy Scouts, nursing homes, art galleries where they teach classes, libraries, friends, relatives....

After removing the contents, I attached 20 adhesive mini hooks and added a necklace to each hook.

When transporting the jewelry cases, I insert a foam sheet as a cushioned divider.

Having 80 necklaces ready to display makes setting up and breaking down go much more quickly.

P.S. A backgammon case could also be transformed into a display case.

Buy an inexpensive art kit with a wood case. Many are available online for under $20.

Remove the art supplies and the plastic inserts. Apply mini adhesive hooks in a straight line.

DIY

NECKLACE CASE

Hang necklaces on the mini hooks.

Keep foam inside case when closed

Use sturdy containers and bags

Imagine hauling your inventory into the venue, your bag breaks, and things scatter everywhere.

Meanwhile, everyone else is unloading and trying to not trip on your items.

Envisioning this scenario is enough to justify purchasing quality bags and other durable containers.

A large bag can easily hold 4 jewelry cases, curtain panels ("tablecloths") and scarves (shelf coverings).

Save time!

Keep necklaces on the display forms while being transported in a handy wood crate.

Get some wheels to save on your heels!

Roll to the show...

A large suitcase with wheels and a pull strap can save trips when setting up and works for storage between shows.

Yes, a wagon that folds up!

Folding wagons may be found in the camping department of stores that *have* camping departments!

My blue wagon has larger wheels than others that I have seen. The wide wheels handle gravel, grass, and other bumpy terrain quite smoothly.

The wagon operates easily. I just pull a tab in the middle to "collapse" the body. It has a removable folding cushion for the bottom.

When you cannot stack your items high enough to justify buying a cart, consider getting a wagon to help you haul.

This folding wagon can hold 200 pounds. It saves trips, so it saves time.

Load your vehicle as much as feasible

the night before the show

Remember: "Last in, first out" when you organize, load, and unload your vehicle. If the craft fair is close enough to your town, you may be able to set up your booth the night before the event, which makes the day of the show less hectic.

Hooray for seats that fold down!

Speed up setting up

Instead of hauling in *everything* from your vehicle before setting up, unpack and organize **one** load at a time. That speeds up the process. Many vendors are trying to get ready simultaneously; most are in a rush. When you have everything waiting to be unpacked and situated, you must find space for your display items and inventory all at once without much work space. If you concentrate on the display props first, it will be easier to add the inventory afterwards.

Experiment and see which system works faster for you.

Set up sped up
when I unpacked
the first wagon load
before getting the next one.

Display helpers

Wire racks are a lightweight way to raise items to make them easier for customers to see. They don't take much room to pack, especially when placed upside down with other containers inside of them. Racks are often found in the kitchen organization sections in stores. Since they were designed to hold heavy dishes and cans of food, they are quite sturdy.

Fishing tackle boxes work well as jewelry cases or as containers for craft supplies. Most have adjustable compartments. They fit nicely inside of the upside down wire racks when being transported.

The plastic storage containers may also be stacked, covered, and used to elevate displays.

Ways to display

Triple layers to triple the interest and maximize the space

Layers to lure more looking

Scarves cover the wire racks supporting the standing jewelry cases. The reclining necklace cases hide the uncovered wire racks which have more necklaces arranged under them. Whether you decide to cover the racks with some sort of fabric may depend on how much light you want underneath them and what you want to showcase.

Contrasts attract attention

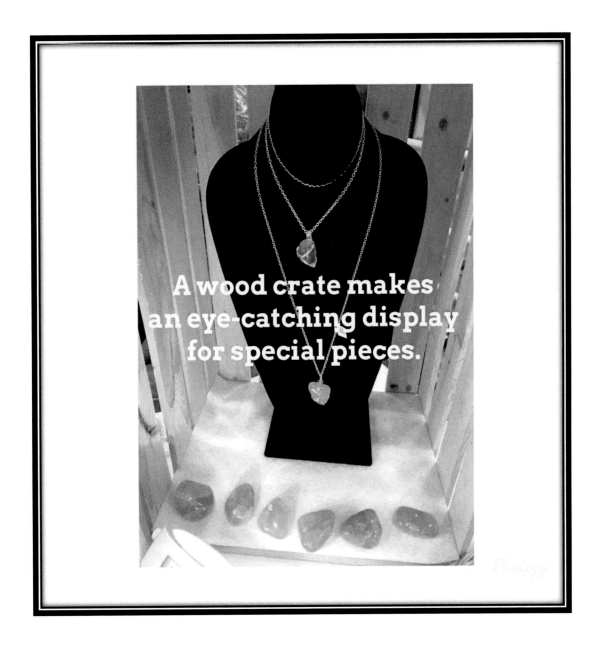

A wood crate makes an eye-catching display for special pieces.

White, glittery felt softens and brightens the unfinished wood crate's bottom. The large, tumbled rose quartz stones enhance the smaller rose quartz and amethyst necklaces on the velvety, black display bust.

More ways to display (to spark more ideas)

The wire backdrop may also be reconfigured into a cube to display items inside it or on top.

Make a U-turn!

A U-shaped space
allows people to browse
more easily.

A U-shaped space is my favorite layout IF the space is wide enough to accommodate two parallel tables and IF people have adequate space to browse on either side and still have enough room to turn around. It invites the customers who are truly interested in your products into your space while making it less tempting for kids to play with your items.

Having two long tables helps divide your emphasis into separate zones. A small table or tray, forming the narrow part of the *U*, functions as the money station.

Lights, luster, luscious!

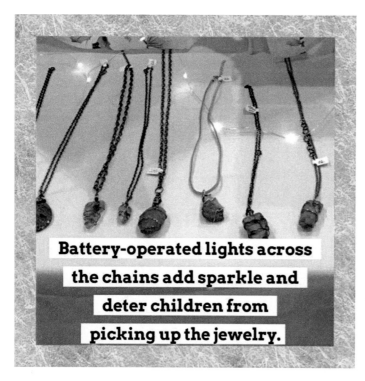

Battery-operated lights across the chains add sparkle and deter children from picking up the jewelry.

Craft fair venues are not known for having excellent lighting for viewing small items on a table. Gymnasiums and other public spaces have lights far overhead. Consequently, battery-operated strings of lights can help your booth shine.

In addition to adding mini lights for their glowing ambiance, they serve another purpose. As truly adorable as children are, some do not understand why they shouldn't play with vendors' displays. Some are kinesthetic learners who like to handle things, and people of all ages naturally like touching pretty things.

Incorporating lights across the necklaces or other products somewhat inhibits the children's inclinations to play with the displays. They seem more content to just look and admire.

The small strand of lights glimmers and encourages people to handle the crystals more carefully.

DRAWSTRING BAGS $3 & $5

Twinkle, twinkle

This was the first time that I used battery-operated lights, and the strand of lights added a soft glow to the bowls of crystals. This table was just part of my pop-up shop selection.

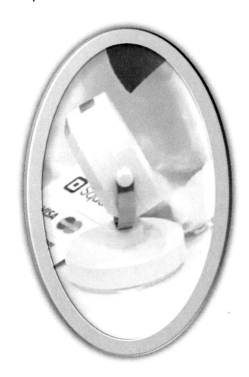

If your booth is in a darker area, mini spotlights also add pizzazz. Battery-operated lights can be set up nearly anywhere, and you don't need to pay extra for a booth with electricity or worry about anyone tripping over the cords.

With jewelry or crystals, *shine is divine!*

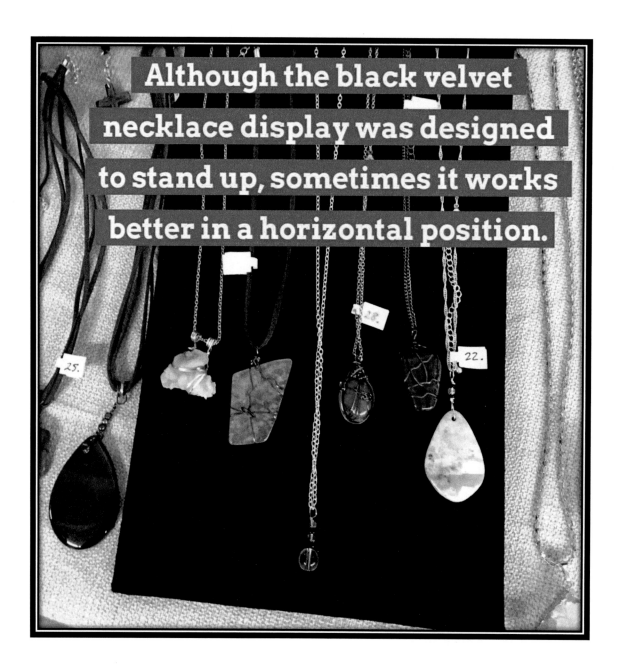

Although the black velvet necklace display was designed to stand up, sometimes it works better in a horizontal position.

The beauty of laying necklaces down is that the lights shine down on the stones and chains better and create a soft, gleaming effect.

An uplifting idea!

Leg Lifts - for Tables

Suggestion: Cut four 12" pieces of **1.5" PVC pipe** and spray paint them.
Insert the table legs into the PVC to raise the table top to approximately 36" high.

Why would someone do this?

1. To elevate merchandise so that people can view it better.
2. To raise the height where the tabletop is not so "handy" for little ones.
3. To reduce strain on your back.

Have multiple tables? Have multiple heights to multiply interest.

Bonus: Use these leg lifts at home when having company to use as a counter-height serving table.

Chicken wire wisdom

A 5' folding chicken wire display will fit into a car with the seats folded down.

Chicken wire weighs less than pegboard, yet is still sturdy. It doesn't block the light either. Pegboard, on the other hand, creates a more solid background that might work better for certain products.

Overall, it's always wonderful to have options.

Woven wood baskets and round wood slices add warmth

An appealing, organized way to display

Symmetry, consistency, and green packaging for their natural granola product

Different directions

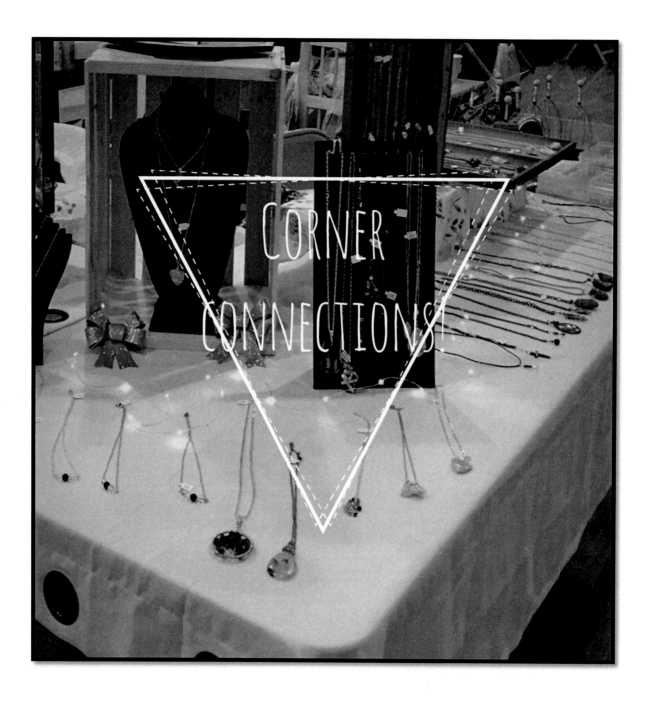

Having an inside **corner spot** with two tables allows for **double exposure**.

Aha: angles!

Line things up!

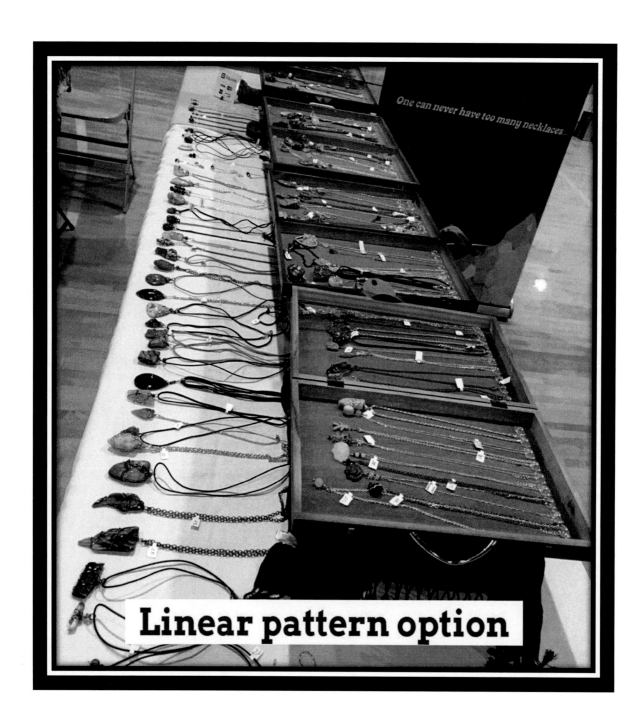

One can never have too many necklaces...

Linear pattern option

Background details

The **wood crate** works to elevate a revolving necklace stand.

The orange **scarves** are a fitting color for a fall event.

It is helpful to have a **variety of colors** on hand to change your fabric coverings to **complement the season.**

Autumn leaves

Instead of holding tea lights, the autumn leaves feature necklaces for a bright twist.

Stack

to

attract

(and to save space)

Spice is nice!

SPICE UP YOUR DISPLAY! BAMBOO OR EXPANDABLE

Spice racks add height and "step up" your customers' viewing focal points. They may be made from bamboo, wood, metal, or plastic.

Multiple goals

Color is one way to catch your customers' initial interest, and **diversity** also lures them in. If you have something that they haven't seen before, they will want to come over and check it out! It's more difficult to get repeat customers if you offer only one type of item, especially if it's something seasonal. You want a **cohesive theme**, but offer more than one thing.

Another example of varying heights, colors and layouts to accommodate that show's venue

afted jewelry
y Brenda DeHa
wagner, SD

many necklaces...

Organize by color and heights.

Group by color or by similar characteristics. These are mainly pale pink rose quartz.

Layers of color

Rainbow colors, multiple heights, and different textures entice customers to notice your booth.

Clear vision

Display cases on a covered folding plastic "bench" to raise them to an easy-to-see level.

Dual purposes

I carried geodes to craft fairs inside a vintage wood tool holder. After unloading them, I flipped the wood case to display cross necklaces. **Whenever you can utilize a carrying case for display, you are saving time and storage space.**

Stick up, flip up, and go!

This clever vendor has a display on an easel that holds many necklaces. When it's time to pack, the bottom flips up to cover the jewelry. The necklaces hang from T-shaped stick pins.

Baskets and more baskets

Be a basket case!
Baskets offer easy,
lightweight options
to organize items.

Multiple baskets

Unity

BASKET BACKDROPS

TO TIE THINGS TOGETHER

A **basket backdrop** unifies groups of similar items and adds texture and interest.

Crystals craze

I sell crystals (a.k.a. rocks!) to demonstrate that each necklace usually started as a tumbled or rough stone before I wrapped wire around it.

I do not tumble the stones; I buy them at rock shops in the Black Hills, at holistic health expos, at an occasional auction, online...or wherever else I can find them.

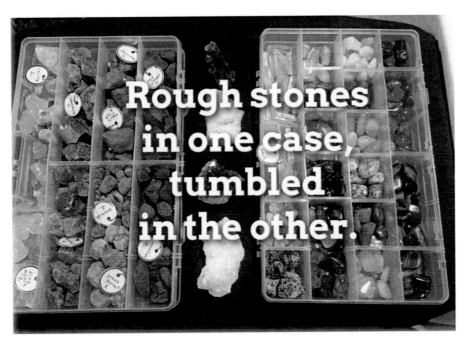

Kids *love* them also and will play with the crystals (instead of with my necklaces).

Variety

Although I've said to organize by color, mixing things up with color is also fun!

Just be creative and see what looks right at each venue.

More variety!

These colorful items are arranged **vertically, horizontally,** and **at angles.**

Easels in varying sizes and designs support an interesting assortment of crosses, inspirational words, and other wood creations.

For some crafts, easels are essential.

Background check!

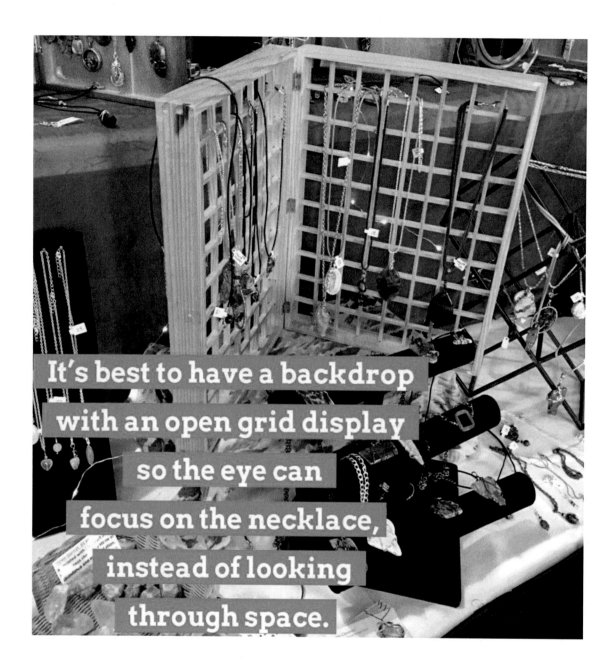

It's best to have a backdrop with an open grid display so the eye can focus on the necklace, instead of looking through space.

If the **open grid** above would *not* have had the blue fabric behind it, the necklaces would have been less noticeable. Our eyes like a "stopping point" when looking at objects surrounded by space. Stores often have a big display when you first enter to give you a spot to start focusing.

Wine time?

The **wine rack display** would benefit from a more solid background, yet its **geometric shape** still makes an interesting arrangement. Larger necklaces work better than smaller pendants in this type of display.

Light vs. dark

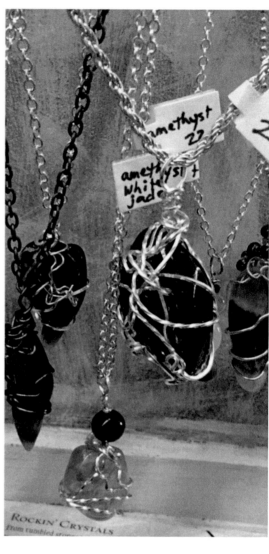

Use a light background for darker colored stones like amethyst.

Generally, use a light background for dark objects and a darker background for lighter-colored objects.

Of course, with creative enterprises,
exceptions may make things…**exceptional!**

Pretty patterns

The mind subconsciously looks for patterns and alignment.

Arranging items in a certain pattern is one way to attract more attention to your products. It provides a **focal point** as well.

Sign time

This hand-painted sign fits their booth's style.

Make your business name known! You want people to know and remember you.

Put ideas into people's heads!

Let them know that you are interested in having a pop-up shop and where else to find your creations.

Although a pop-up shop is usually held in someone else's retail business, one may be set up in all kinds of places, even outdoors. Many public spaces will accommodate a pop-up shop, and sometimes people set up shop in their own homes.

Shop local...shop small...shop 'til you drop...just shop!

Encourage people to shop and to support local businesses...like *your* business!

Gifts of gratitude

Remind them of the special helpers in their lives.

It doesn't have to be a holiday or someone's birthday to give them a present; thank you or "thinking of you" gifts show meaningful appreciation.

Seasonal fairs

SEASONAL ITEMS
FUN BUT LIMITED
SALES WINDOW

Holiday napkins add festivity.

Santa and kids

Many parents bring their children to fairs that offer pictures with Santa. That's a good thing!

The minor downside is that a *few* of those children want to rearrange your booth's items if not redirected. If the parents don't caution their children to "just look, don't touch," then don't be afraid to protect your displays.

One little girl took her hand and dragged it along a row of my necklaces to push them into one big pile. Her mom, talking (and *talking*) to the vendor in the next booth, never noticed.

Another incident, a boy ran raced through the space behind my booth and slid (flew!) lickety-split under my table to scare a girl who was looking at necklaces on the other side. It happened so fast that all I could exclaim was *"No!"* Both kids quickly disappeared after that incident. Luckily, it all turned out fine.

Remember, kids who like craft fairs turn into adults who like craft fairs.

Santa = kids
(lots of kids)

"O Christmas Tree…"

Patterns…

Again,
patterns can
make displays
instinctively "click"
for
people.

After the holidays...

If something seasonal doesn't sell and you do not want to hold onto it for another year, take it apart and make something else with it. You get the joy of creation once again!

Recycle/upcycle seasonal items when feasible.

Wreaths...always welcoming!

Wreaths are not just for Christmas. This year-round craft requires a lot of room, both for storing and transporting. The hard plastic wreath containers make it easy to stack them. Check secondhand stores periodically for these helpers.

Flexible plastic wreath storage containers have handles helpful for when you carry them. They also protect the wreaths.

And there are always heavy-duty lawn and leaf bags. Whatever works!

Little and lively!

Round table, round merchandise!

Small tables and TV trays initiate little islands of interest.

With plastic tabletops, they are lighter to carry but are still sturdy enough for items up to approximately 30 pounds.

They provide another viewing zone to expand your merchandise areas and traffic flows.

A small folding tray is lightweight and features an additional display area.

Behind the scenes...

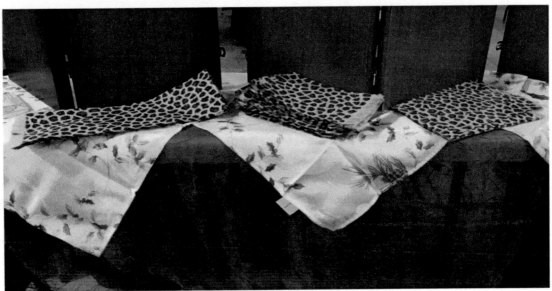

Hideaway

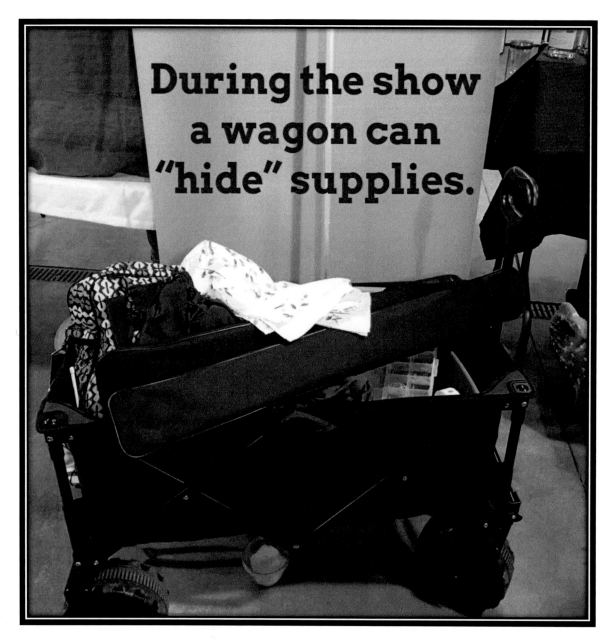

During the show a wagon can "hide" supplies.

Most of the time I store extra bags and items under the table, but the banner and table together hid the wagon and its contents at this fair.

The beauty of a long tablecloth is that you may hide your containers, bags, and extra supplies. You want the tablecloth as long as feasible on the customers' side and shorter on your side so that you may both hide and *find* things more easily.

Comfort zone

Wear comfortable shoes, layers of clothing to adapt to the room's temperature, and sit down when you can. The preparations and actual show can be hard on your back and your feet.

Bring a refillable water bottle to stay hydrated and snacks, especially if no other food will be available.

Sometimes the best spot for your chair is beside your display.

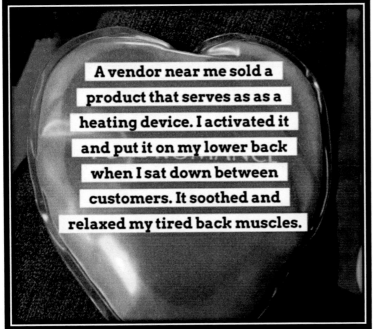

A vendor near me sold a product that serves as as a heating device. I activated it and put it on my lower back when I sat down between customers. It soothed and relaxed my tired back muscles.

Hand warmers could also warm your lower back to ease sore muscles.

Mirror images

Mirror, mirror...

Who forgot the mirror?!

A jewelry booth should have a mirror, one that is durable enough to travel and be handled frequently. After all, you want people to try on necklaces to get them more inclined to purchase them.

If you forget a mirror, tell your customers to put their phone cameras on **"selfie" mode**. This feature will work as a temporary mirror of how they look modeling the necklaces.

#SELFIE

A selfie serves as an impromtu mirror when needed.

Door prizes and swag bag gifts

I had a booth for three days at the South Dakota Yoga Conference. Vendors were asked to contribute something to be inserted into 125 swag bags. I spelled *YOGA* with crystals, designed coupons, and hired the local print shop to copy them.

For door prizes and swag bag gifts, I offer **gift certificates** or **coupons**. These get people to your booth, and then they may select what they like the best. They might buy more also.

Occasionally, the vendor application information will state that they'd like door prizes worth a certain dollar amount. Most of the events leave the amounts up to each vendor.

Picture this…and *this*…and that!

Photographs are helpful for keeping track of your inventory, for marketing on social media, and for refreshing your memory!

I'd stayed up too late the night before the South Dakota Yoga Conference. I kept making "just one more necklace" and didn't get everything done.

As my husband drove, I priced and photographed my latest jewelry. I needed a background while cruising 80 m.p.h. down I-90 (the legal speed limit, by the way). I found a map in the glove compartment, and it became my backdrop. The drive took hours, and it took me hours to do all this.

TAKE PICTURES.

YOU'LL BE GLAD LATER.

And share those pictures!

Sneak peek!

chryscolla

amethyst

seraphinite

POST PICTURES ON SOCIAL MEDIA TO SHOW THE PROCESS.

People engage on **social media** to see what others are doing, to get updates on their daily lives. Sharing your handiwork is a natural expression of your interests. These are positive posts, and people like seeing them.

Favorites?

Whenever I share pictures of my new necklaces, people seem to prefer one item over the others. I can rarely predict which one will be the favorite. It's enlightening to see which style people prefer.

In addition to personal social media accounts, consider setting up business pages if you have not already done so. My Rockin' Crystals Facebook page is public so that more than just my friends and family can view my jewelry.

Social media is **free marketing**; take advantage of it.

Pricing: one of the not-so-exciting parts

How much?!

It can be very perplexing to know how much to charge. After all, you aren't in the business to lose money! It's a balancing act between your time, your product expenses, and actual profit.

One way to start the pricing process is to ask honest, tactful friends how much they would be willing to pay if purchasing these same items from a stranger. Similar items should have the same or very similar prices. If some items are more expensive, be able to explain why if someone would ask. Have a range of price points to fit more people's budgets, which results in more sales.

I have tried a variety of price tags. The stringed ones caused too many tangles. Also, I allow people to trade chains if they'd like; tags with strings complicated things. I now use adhesive labels marketed as jewelry repair and identification tags. Just keep experimenting until you find one that works best for your items.

Price tags: started with strings, now use adhesive labels.

Circle this!

For an occasional item, the "key tag" works as a price tag. The round shape accents the round beaded earrings made by one of my students. She is interested in craft fairs, helped me set up my booth at one fair, and I sold her earrings for her.

I used these as price tags, but their size overshadowed the pendants.

Large tags

These larger price tags are attached to the chicken wire with clothes pins.

Pricing time saver

Some items may all be priced the same, which saves time.

Retail world

This vendor sells fresh granola in a local and area stores.

More store displays

Location matters. A glass ginger jar or a vintage lamp shade wouldn't travel well, but these showcase necklaces nicely between craft fairs while at a store.

The ginger jar makes a captivating holder with necklaces on the outside and an informational card on the inside of the jar.

Since it was difficult to have a background directly behind the necklaces on the lamp shade, larger pendants in earth tones were chosen so they wouldn't be "lost in space."   A vintage lamp shade requires a fair amount of space, but the interesting lines and patina create an intriguing stationary display.

Suggestions for craft fair organizers

*Don't schedule your event really close to other craft fairs in your town or area.

You share the same customer base in town, so events need to be spread out. In a small town, guests may attend every event in the vicinity, but they will probably buy only one time at your booth when the events are close together and they see the same merchandise.

*Please clarify the size of the tables provided in each booth.

Most events, if providing tables, use either 6' or 8' long tables. If both sizes will be at the fair, a booth with a 6' table could cost $5 less than an 8' table. (In South Dakota, your vendor booth fee usually includes one table.)

When I have been at shows with two table lengths, I have been assigned a 6' table while someone with fewer items received an 8' table. At one show, a vendor with an 8' table didn't show up while I had everything condensed on a 6' table.

Granted, the craft fair committee members have no idea how much inventory the vendors will bring; that is why the table sizes should be clearly explained with the application information.

*If you have a concession stand, have someone take and deliver food orders to the vendors.

*Advertise heavily in papers and on social media.

Create a public event on Facebook and encourage vendors to post pictures and share the event page. Create posters for the town's stores and e-mail the poster as an attachment to out-of-town vendors to post.

*If vendors bring their children for the day, encourage them in the vendor information to keep their children occupied at *their own* booths.

One vendor had a two-level display of tables covered with long tablecloths, which made a "fort." Her three children played quietly for hours underneath the tables. Customers had no idea that kids were nearby.

Another vendor brings her grandsons, and the boys sell their own items at a special area in the same booth. They craft together, and they make memories and money together.

*If it's a kid-friendly event like taking Santa pictures, have organized activities for the kids while they wait.

Girl Scouts, FCCLA, or other teen groups could have crafting "Make & Take" tables, games, or story time in a separate area. Many facilities don't have the space for this, but some do.

*Small town craft fairs are essentially over by 2:00 or 2:30. End them then.

*Visit the vendors' booths.

During the fair, it's gratifying when organizers stop by the booth to see how things are going and to thank you for coming. Most craft fairs are a fundraiser for an organization, and vendors are a big part of helping to raise those funds. A brief visit gives the vendor an opportunity to thank the "hosts" also. The committee goes to a tremendous amount of work organizing, setting up, and breaking down the event. Overall, an event is a team effort with mutual benefits.

*Follow up with feedback.

Everyone wants the event to be a success—the organizers, the vendors, the customers, and the townspeople. Have a survey for vendors to complete—or just ask when you visit with them. Vendors have different levels of experience and different tips to share to make the event as wonderful as (realistically) possible.

Progress, not perfection!

I have come a long way from the beginning of my crafting life, whether at a fair or with online sales. I sell mainly custom jewelry at my Rockin' Crystals Etsy store, www.rockincrystals.etsy.com, because it's easier than uploading everything online and then deleting an item when it sells at a craft fair or at a consignment store. My Rockin' Crystals Etsy store shows examples of necklaces that I take to craft fairs. Customers pick a style that they like and request me to make something similar according to their preferences.

I have other jewelry that I send to Crystal Vaults in Florida. They market it and sell it on consignment through their website. Like it or not, people do shop online for various reasons, such as avoiding city congestion or living in isolated areas. Consequently, you can expand your craft fair business by selling online.

Versatility is vital. Each show has a different venue, so that often calls for a different display layout, even if the basics remain the same.

Always add to your inventory. At my first craft fair, I *thought* I had a lot of necklaces and earrings at the time. I did not. Adding to your product line is part of the evolution of your business. Currently, I take over 100 necklaces to shows, as well as bringing other items (that I didn't make) to increase variety and decrease some price points.

If there were a magic formula for becoming rich crafters, we'd all be rich crafters. Since there's not, just enjoy the process. Know that there are cycles, and things will never be perfect. Of course, you'd like to be in it for the money; fortunately, creating offers its own rewards. You will be enriched through the "natural high" of creating, by the camaraderie with your fellow vendors, and with selling enough products to keep your business evolving. And some people do "make it big." I hope that you will be one of them!

Finally...

THE NOT-SO-FUN ASPECTS OF A CRAFTING BUSINESS
Clutter Control

The dumping ground   The goal

Now that I have a lull between craft fairs and have finished this book, it's time to clean my poor jewelry station again. The biggest problem is that once I have enough space to create something (I'm talking a placemat size!), I end up making "just one necklace" instead of sorting and putting everything away first. *HELP!*

How this book happened…

Brenda DeHaan intended to write just a pamphlet on how to create jewelry display cases from art supply kits to help fellow vendors. It was going to be available through her Rockin' Crystals Etsy store. However, she couldn't seem to stop writing and eventually ended up with this book. She hopes that the common sense information compiled here will be both helpful and inspirational.

Writing it was so much fun that she had to write another book, *Crafty Decluttering*. As you can probably guess from the previous page, her craft room needed help—some serious help. Writing a book about the process was the motivation she needed to declutter.

She is currently working on *Rockin' Crystals*, a book about her fascinating journey with healing crystals. Written in a down-to-earth style, this book explains the basics of crystal healing and how it can enhance lives. *Rockin' Crystals* should be published during the fall of 2018.

Made in the USA
San Bernardino, CA
14 August 2018